Cats of the World

Big and Small Color Them All

A fun coloring experience for all

Loretta Emmons

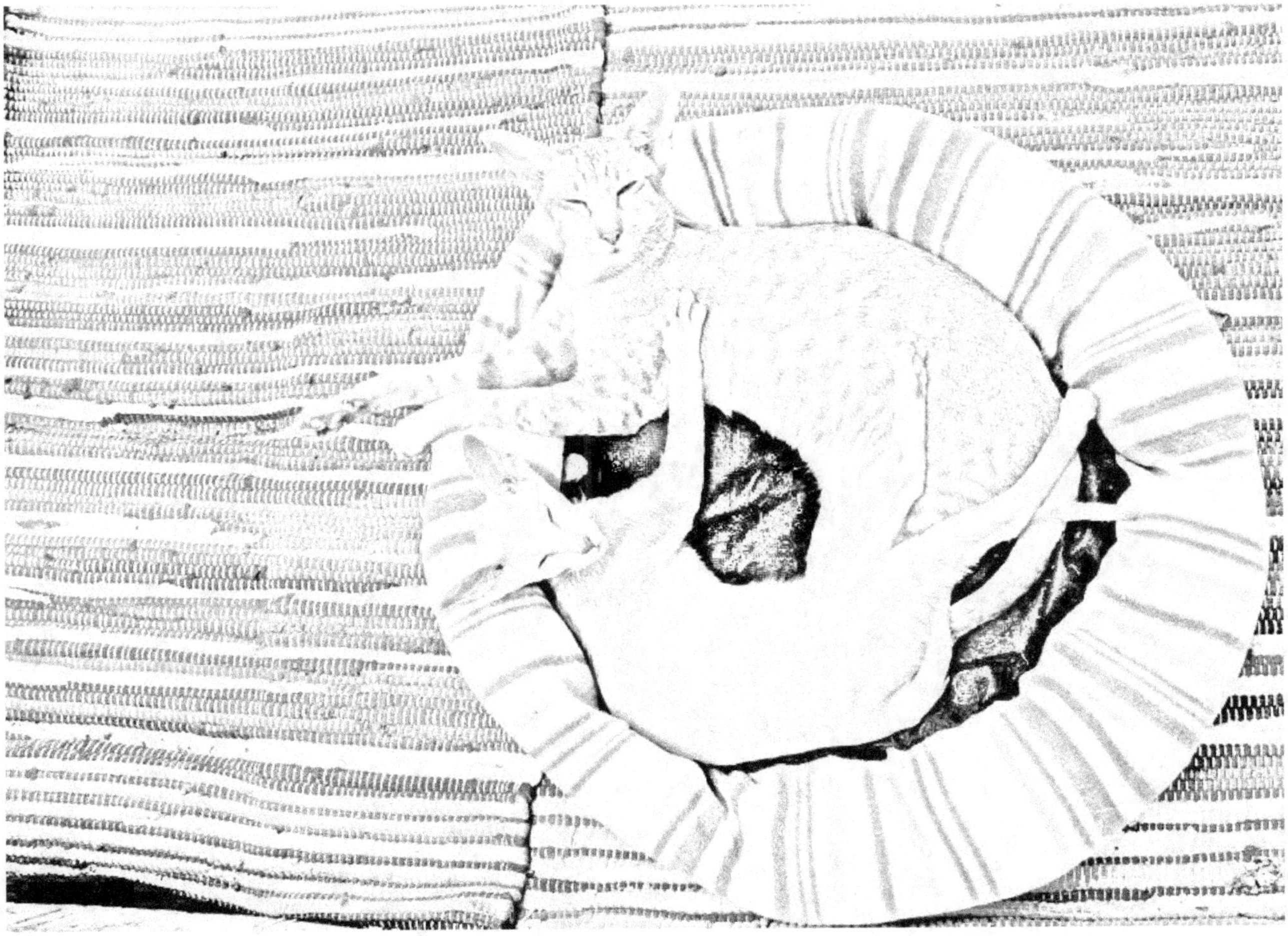

www.ingramcontent.com/pod-product-compliance
Lightning Source LLC
Chambersburg PA
CBHW081408280526
45788CB00009B/3028
* 9 7 8 1 5 4 2 8 3 4 6 2 9 *